Contents

Page

Page

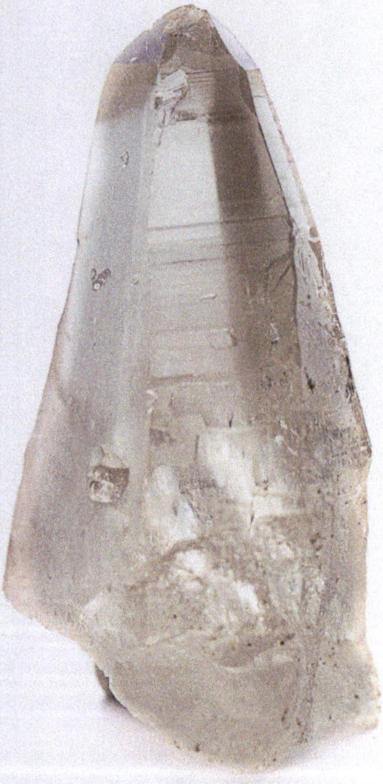

This Crystal book o' notes belongs to

....

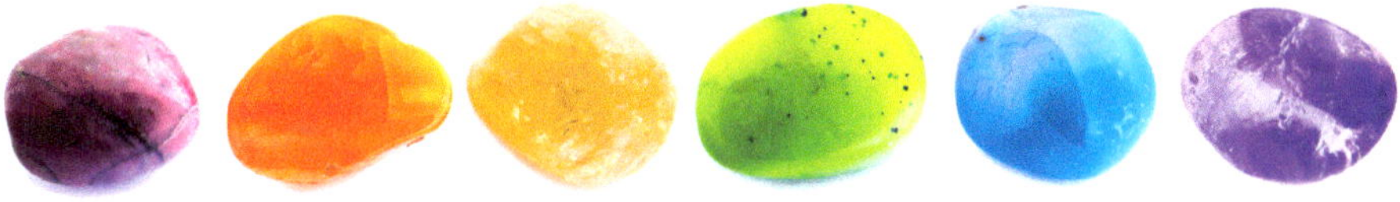

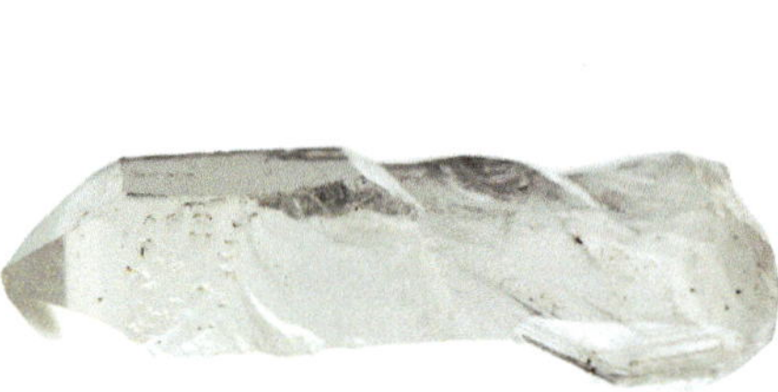

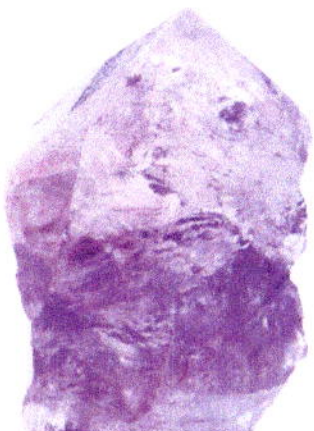

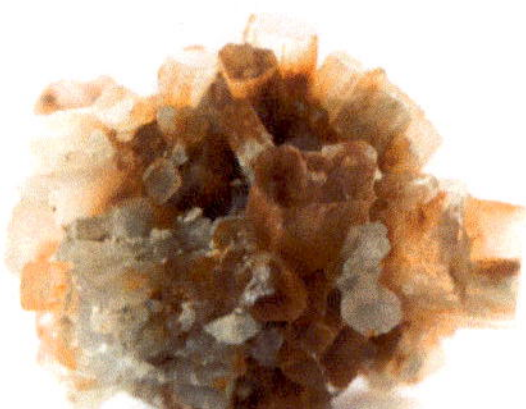

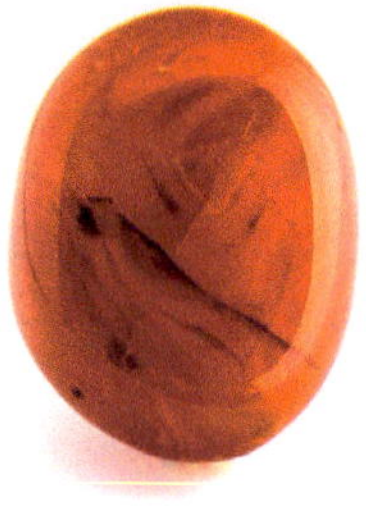

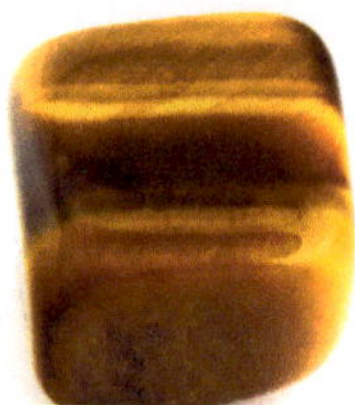

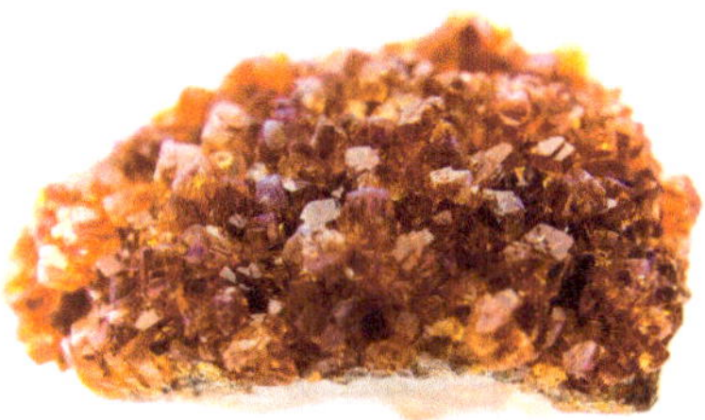

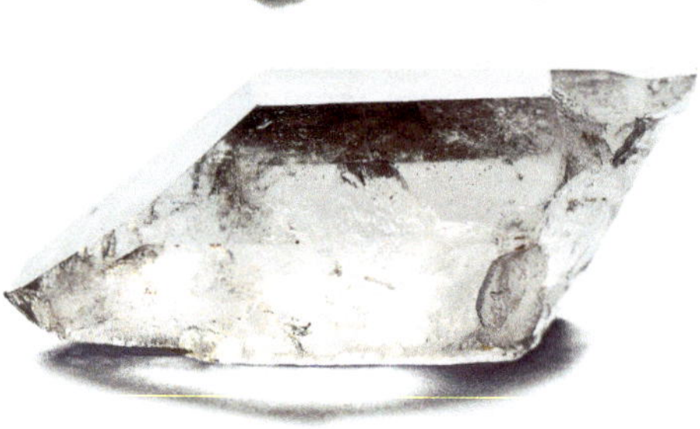

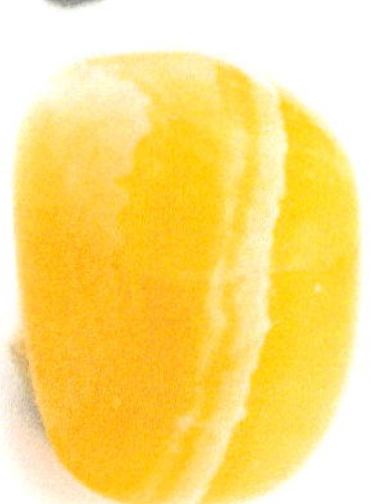

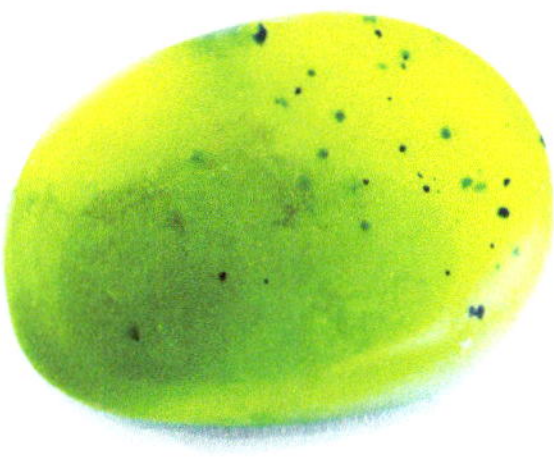

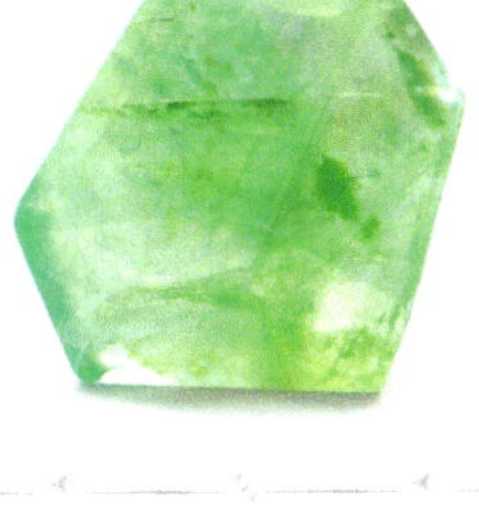

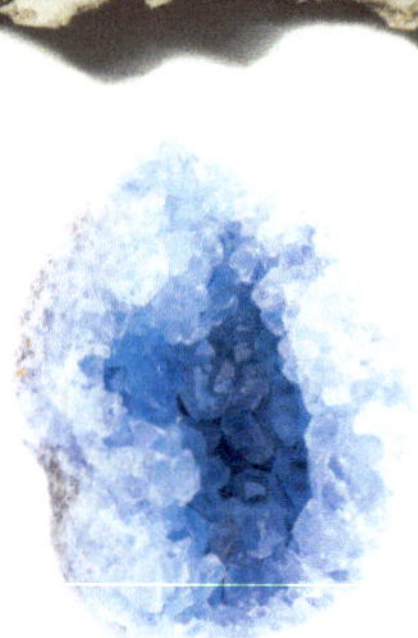

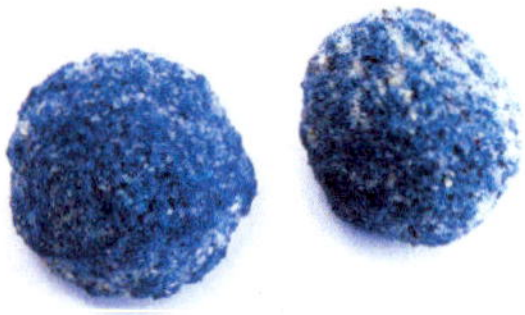

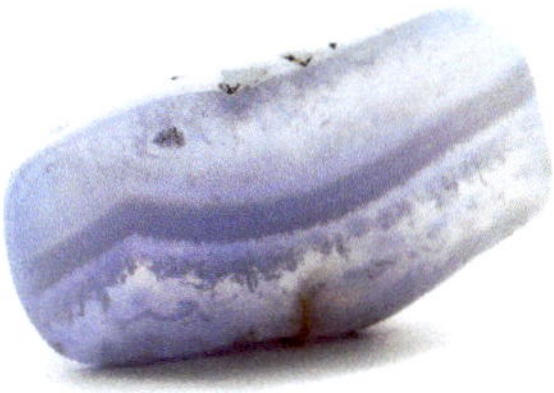

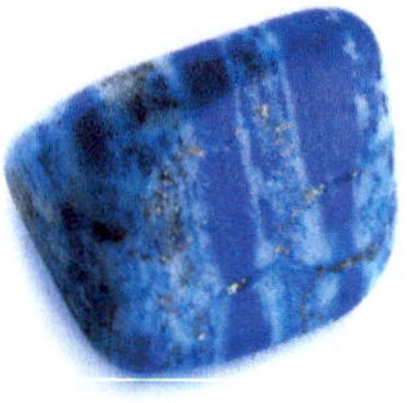

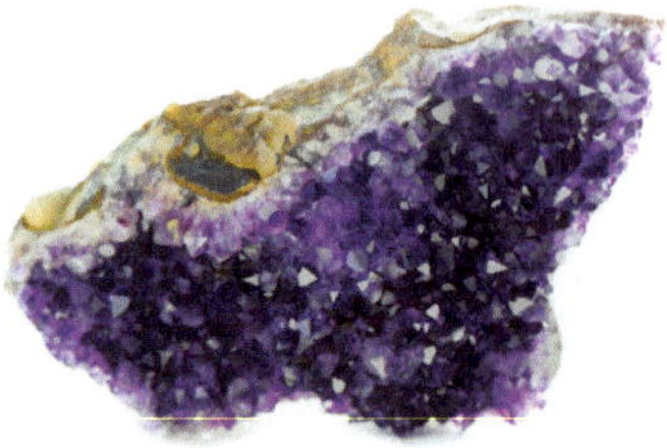

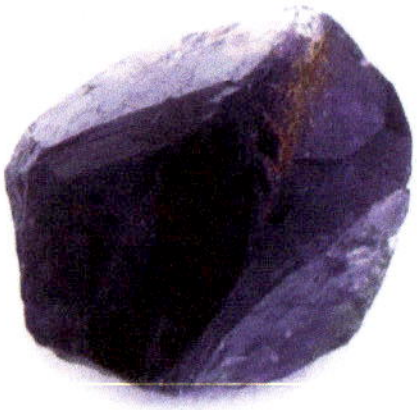

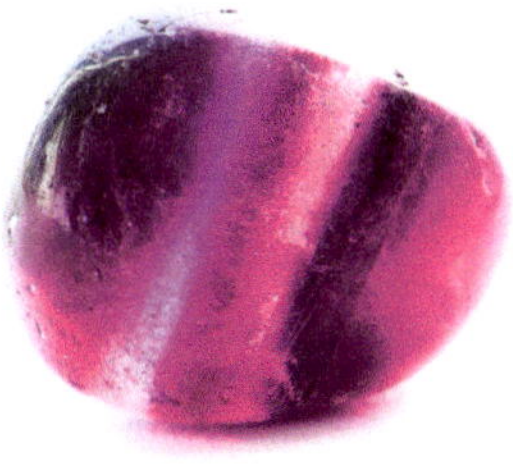

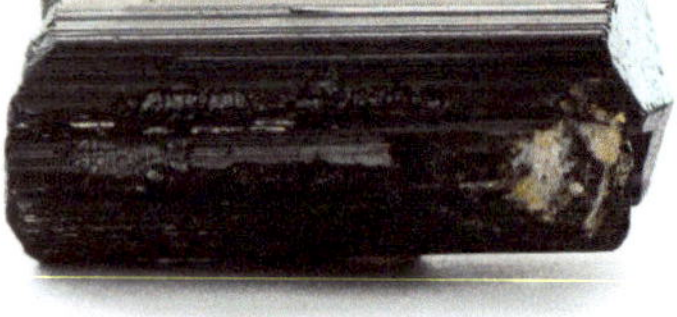

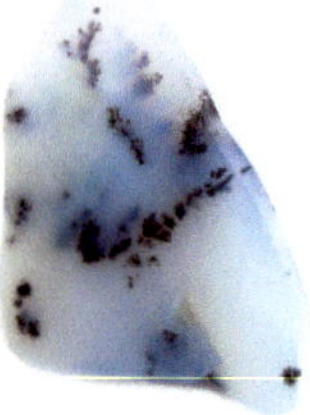

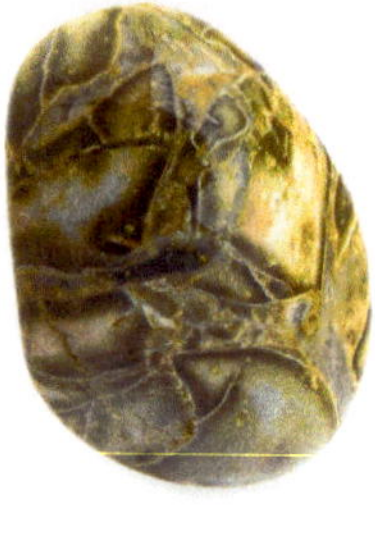

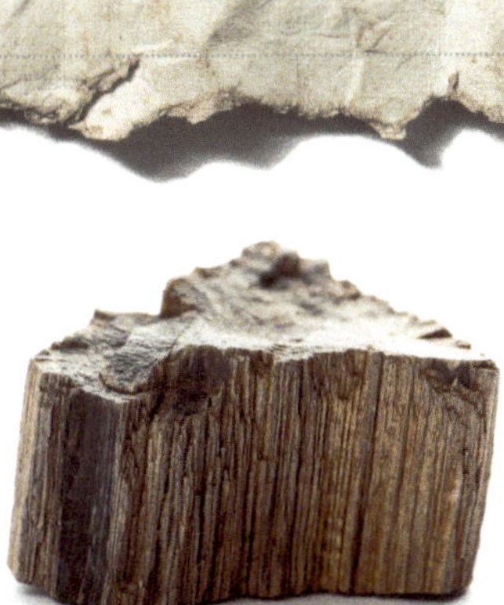

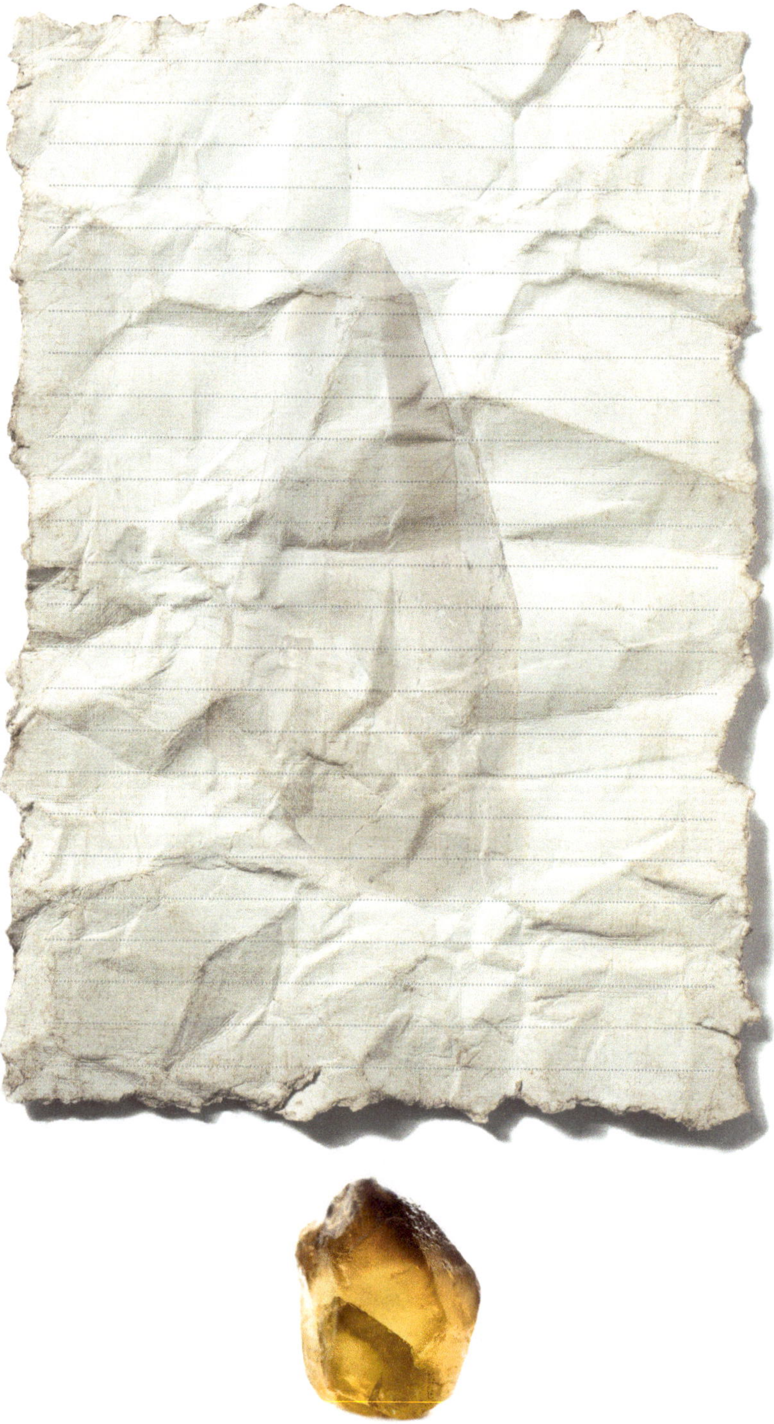

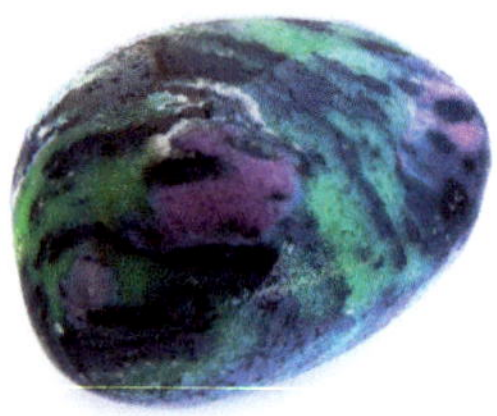

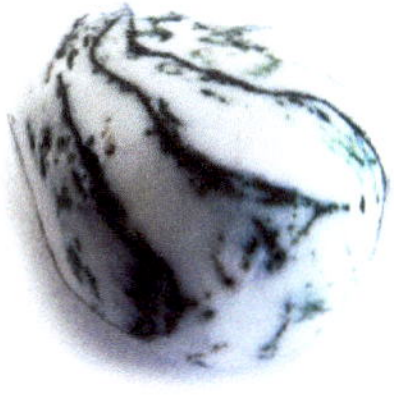

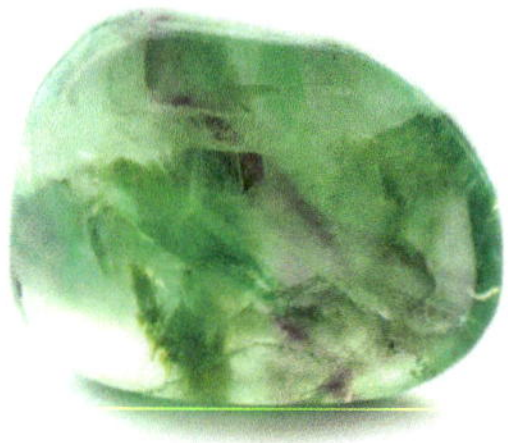

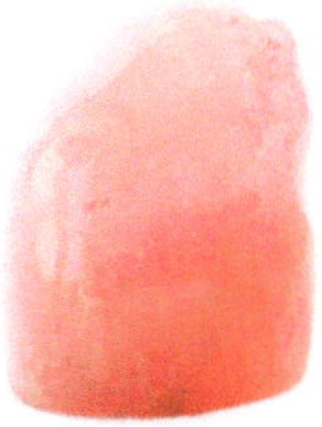

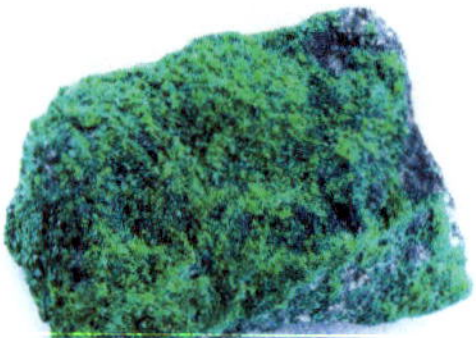

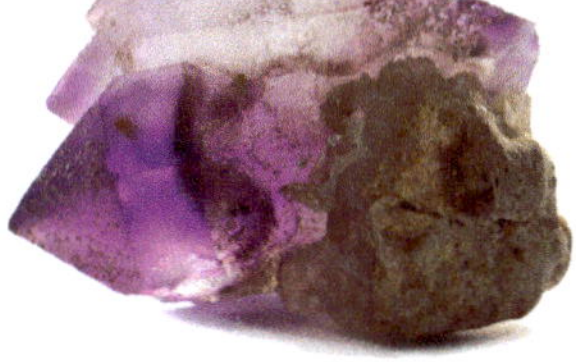

www.ingramcontent.com/pod-product-compliance
Lightning Source LLC
Chambersburg PA
CBHW040938030426
42335CB00001B/39
* 9 7 8 1 9 2 2 4 1 5 2 0 2 *